**DATE DUE**

# WWI
# EVENTS LEADING TO WORLD WAR I

## JOHN HAMILTON

# VISIT US AT
## WWW.ABDOPUB.COM

Published by ABDO & Daughters, an imprint of ABDO Publishing Company, 4940 Viking Drive, Suite 622, Edina, Minnesota 55435. Copyright ©2004 by Abdo Consulting Group, Inc. International copyrights reserved in all countries. No part of this book may be reproduced in any form without written permission from the publisher.

Printed in the United States.

Edited by Jessica Klein
Graphic Design: John Hamilton
Cover Design: Mighty Media
Photos and illustrations:
    Corbis, p. 1, 4-9, 12, 14-29
    Photos of the Great War, p. 8, 28
    John Hamilton, p. 10-11, 13
    *Cover photo:* Corbis

**Library of Congress Cataloging-in-Publication Data**

Hamilton, John, 1959-
    Events leading to World War I / John Hamilton.
    p. cm.—(World War I)
    Includes index.
    Summary: An overview of the causes of World War I.
    ISBN 1-57765-914-7
    1. World War, 1914-1918—Causes—Juvenile literature. 2. Arms race—Europe—History—20th century—Juvenile literature. [1. World War, 1914-1918—Causes.] I. Title: Events leading to World War One. II. Title.

D511. H24 2003
940.3'11—dc21

2002033295

# TABLE OF CONTENTS

# THE WAR TO END ALL WARS

*Far right:* A soldier observes the ruins of a church after a battle in 1918. *Below:* Artist Louis Raemaekers painted this scene of a World War I battlefield.

**ON JUNE 28, 1914,** an assassin's bullet cut down the heir to the throne of Austria-Hungary. The victim was Archduke Franz Ferdinand. His country had recently added Bosnia-Herzegovina to its empire. He had been visiting Bosnia-Herzegovina's capital, Sarajevo, when he was killed, along with his wife, Sophie von Hohenberg.

Bosnia-Herzegovina is in southeastern Europe, in an area known as the Balkans. It had seen two previous wars in 1912 and 1913. The killing of the archduke began a third conflict, but this time events spiraled out of control, plunging Europe, and eventually the world, into a war of unbelievable horror and destruction.

Before the war began, two armed sides squared off against each other. The Triple Alliance was made up of Germany, Austria-Hungary, and Italy. The Triple Entente, also called the Allies, included France, Russia, and Great Britain. Each of these countries had a complicated web of alliances among themselves and other minor countries, each agreeing to come to the aid of the other if one was attacked. The alliances became a trap, dooming most of the world to four years of war more horrible than anyone had ever expected.

By the time it was over in 1918, nearly 15 million people had lost their lives. Another 21 million soldiers were wounded. A conflict that started between a handful of powerful European countries grew to affect nearly every country in the world. The war caused unimaginable destruction and misery.

At the time, the conflict was called the Great War. Today we call it World War I. It was hard to believe that any war could be worse than World War I. It was so terrible that most people thought the world would have learned its lesson. That's why it was also called "the war to end all wars." But less than 20 years later, World War II erupted, spreading death and devastation on an even greater scale.

Most people know a lot more about World War II than the Great War. In many ways, World War I caused World War II. It created the conditions that gave rise to Adolph Hitler and Nazi Germany. World War II is often described as the worldwide struggle of good versus evil. The causes of World War I are more difficult to understand. Sitting in the comfort of our homes almost 100 years later, it is easy to look back and wonder why the leaders of the world could not have prevented the war. But it's not as simple as that. To truly understand the Second World War, the catastrophe that shaped much of the history of the twentieth century, we first must understand World War I.

*Far right:* British soldiers rest in a French village before being sent into battle.
*Below:* A battle between troops from Austria-Hungary and Italy

# EMPIRES

*Above:* A cartoon shows the major powers as they fight over control of the world.
*Facing page:* Germany's Kaiser Wilhelm II, right, walks with his generals and their staff during WWI.
*Below:* The rise of nationalism was one of the reasons the world went to war in 1914.

**DURING THE FIRST PART** of the twentieth century, Europe seemed calm. The continent as a whole hadn't seen war since Napoleon Bonaparte ruled France nearly 100 years earlier. Under the surface, however, hostility was boiling between Europe's superpowers. These included Britain, France, Germany, Austria-Hungary, and Russia. Each country had its own empire, countries in other parts of the world that it controlled. Britain, France, and Germany competed for trade and military power overseas. Russia and Austria-Hungary were pitted against each other for control of the Balkan countries of southeastern Europe.

All the major countries of Europe had amassed huge armies. The leaders claimed their armed forces were for self-defense. Yet each was convinced that their rivals' armies were really meant as tools for invasion. The rise of nationalism meant that each country wanted more status for itself—more trade, more power, and more territory. By 1914 this national greed would send the world into war.

# EUROPE ON THE EVE OF WWI, 1914

NORWAY

SWEDEN

FINLAND

Atlantic
Ocean

IRELAND

North
Sea

Baltic
Sea

DENMARK

GREAT
BRITAIN

London

English Channel

THE NETHERLANDS

BELGIUM

LUX.

Berlin

GERMANY

Paris

Bay of
Biscay

FRANCE

SWITZERLAND

Vienna

AUSTRIA-
HUNGARY

ITALY

PORTUGAL

Madrid

Sarajevo

MONTE-
NEGRO

SERBIA

ALBANIA

Adriatic Sea

GREECE

SPAIN

CORSICA

Rome

SARDINIA

SPANISH MOROCCO

FRENCH
MOROCCO

ALGERIA

TUNISIA

SICILY

MALTA

Mediterranean Sea

Moscow

RUSSIA

Caspian
Sea

Black Sea

OTTOMAN EMPIRE
(TURKEY)

PERSIA

CYPRUS

ARABIA

11

## GERMANY

The German Empire was formed in 1871. Before then it was a loose collection of small states and principalities. The largest and most powerful of these was Prussia. Otto von Bismarck was Prussia's prime minister, and it was his dream to unite all the German states. He did this through strong-willed diplomacy, and by waging war against Austria-Hungary and France.

Victory in the 1866 Seven Weeks War against Austria-Hungary meant that a collection of northern German states were now controlled by Prussia instead of Austria-Hungary. Bismarck drew the remaining southern German states into the union by provoking a war with France in 1870-1871.

The Franco-Prussian War resulted in a stinging defeat for France. It was forced to give the rich eastern provinces of Alsace and Lorraine to Prussia. The southern German states

*Below:* A group portrait of German soldiers from World War I, including future Nazi dictator Adolf Hitler (seated, left)

joined Prussia and the northern states, creating the German Empire in 1871. France and the rest of Europe were shocked at this shift in the balance of power. During the next 30 years Germany built itself into an industrial giant, second only to the United States and Great Britain.

Wilhelm II became kaiser, or emperor, of Germany in 1888. He wanted to show his European neighbors that Germany was a power to be reckoned with. He was aggressive and arrogant, and his attempts to turn Germany into a world superpower alarmed France and Great Britain.

*Above:* A map showing the disputed region of Alsace-Lorraine.

### FRANCE

After the Franco-Prussian War, France's national pride was deeply hurt. As a prize, the victorious Germans had taken the regions of Alsace and Lorraine. France wanted revenge. To overcome its national humiliation, France wanted Alsace-Lorraine back.

The loss to Germany in the Franco-Prussian War made the French mistrustful of the German people. The French kept a large army on their eastern border to protect themselves against another German invasion. In response, the Germans became more and more suspicious of the French. The Germans suspected that someday the French would try to take back Alsace-Lorraine.

### AUSTRIA-HUNGARY

By 1914 the Austro-Hungarian Empire was a shadow of its former self. Austria-Hungary was a collection of countries and people who over the years had less and less in common with each other. The Seven Weeks War with Prussia in 1866 had weakened the empire. By the turn of the century, Austria-Hungary was trying to hang on to what little influence and power it had left.

Austria-Hungary controlled several countries in the Balkan region. But many people in the Balkans didn't want to be ruled by outsiders anymore. Austria-Hungary became desperate to control its empire and keep it from breaking apart. Its reaction to the killing of Archduke Ferdinand during a visit to Sarajevo in 1914 set off a chain reaction that started World War I.

## RUSSIA

In many ways Russia was like Austria-Hungary at the dawn of World War I. It was an ancient monarchy, but change was in the air. Its people were not happy, and revolution was coming. Tsar Nicholas II tried desperately to regain glory for his country so he could hold on to his throne.

Russia had suffered a humiliating defeat to Japan during the Russo-Japanese War of 1904-1905. To regain prestige for his country, Nicholas II wanted to control and influence countries in the Baltic region, at the expense of Russia's old enemy Turkey. Russia especially wanted control of the Dardanelles area so it could have a secure shipping lifeline and station its warships in the region. By meddling in the Balkans, Russia set itself on a collision course with Austria-Hungary, which also wanted to control the area.

## GREAT BRITAIN

*Below:* British soldiers raise their helmets for the camera as they head toward the trenches in France.

By 1914 Great Britain had built a huge empire of colonies in Africa, India, and Asia. The British economy benefited greatly by controlling the goods and resources of these far-flung imperial colonies.

Although Great Britain didn't have any plans to conquer territory in Europe, it needed the countries of Europe to be stable and at peace so Britain could continue exploiting its own empire. The formation of the German Empire, with its alarming growth and aggressive military buildup, scared many in Great Britain. If the British Empire was to survive, many believed that Germany would have to be stopped, with force if necessary.

## THE UNITED STATES

On the eve of the Great War, the United States was happy to stay out of the fight. It was isolated from Europe by a vast ocean, and the concerns of the European empires seemed out of touch with American interests. Why should the United States fight a European war? Woodrow Wilson won a second term as president in 1916 by campaigning with the slogan, "He kept us out of war."

But the United States was more connected to world affairs than it first thought. It had a huge number of European immigrants, which affected how the country viewed international events. And much of the United States' trade depended on free access to Europe and its colonies. The war hampered U.S. trade and put American lives in danger.

President Wilson struggled to maintain neutrality, but by 1917 the United States would find itself dragged into the war along with the rest of the world.

*Below*: Fresh soldiers from New York board a train to Camp Upton to begin training for fighting in Europe.

# ALLIANCES

*Above:* A soldier says farewell to a loved one as he heads off to war.
*Far right:* A French poster urges citizens to loan money to the government by purchasing war bonds.
*Below:* Italian troops guard a trench in the mountains near Trentino, Italy.

**BECAUSE OF THE UNSTABLE** political situation, and because the threat of war was ever present, most countries in Europe tried to protect themselves from attack by making alliances with other governments. For 50 years prior to World War I, Europe wove a web of tangled alliances that drove most countries into two opposing camps, with upstart powerhouse Germany seemingly at the center of the struggle.

Many of the alliances were based on trade, or military defense. The most dangerous alliances called for one country's army to come to the aid of the other if that country were ever attacked. While on the surface it seemed such alliances made a country safer and stronger, in fact it had just the opposite effect. With the smallest attack or threat by any country, most of Europe would be thrown into war, and that is exactly what happened on June 28, 1914.

When Archduke Franz Ferdinand of Austria-Hungary was murdered while visiting the Bosnia-Herzegovina capital of Sarajevo, suspicion immediately fell on Serb terrorists. Serbia, a neighboring Balkan country, wanted Austria-Hungary out of the region. What happened next was a chain reaction of alliances, with most of Europe going to war like a row of falling dominos.

*Above:* A cheering group of soldiers lifts anchor and heads to war in France.

First Austria-Hungary declared war on Serbia on July 28, 1914. Then, because Russia had a treaty with Serbia, it prepared its huge army for war. This is called mobilization. Once an army is in the process of being mobilized, it is very difficult to stop, almost like a machine with no *off* switch.

Germany was greatly alarmed by Russia's actions. It felt sure that Russia was about to go to war with Germany's ally, Austria-Hungary. On August 1, 1914, Germany declared war on Russia.

The French, meanwhile, had a treaty with Russia that stated each country would come to the other's aid if attacked. Since Germany had declared war on Russia, France started mobilizing its army in support of its ally. And in response to that, on August 3, 1914, Germany declared war on France.

Great Britain had an understanding, or entente, with France. It wasn't required to fight, but its colonial empire would benefit if Germany lost the war. Great Britain also had a treaty to protect Belgium. That small country, resting

between the northern parts of France and Germany, wanted to remain neutral, and Great Britain wanted to keep it that way. Belgium had very important seaports that Great Britain didn't want to fall into German hands. When Germany bullied its way through Belgium on its way to invading France, Great Britain joined the fight and declared war on Germany on August 4, 1914.

Japan had a military alliance with Great Britain, and joined the war three weeks later. The Ottoman Empire, also called Turkey, soon joined forces with Germany and Austria-Hungary to form what was called the Central Powers.

Italy had left the Triple Alliance in 1914. Italy and the United States managed to remain neutral during the first years of the war. But Italy entered the fight in 1915, joining sides with the Allies against Germany. The United States finally went to war in 1917 for several reasons, most importantly as a response to German aggression.

In a nutshell, because a minor leader of a teetering empire was murdered in the backwaters of southeastern Europe, the whole world was propelled headlong into war.

People's idea of war was different back then; most thought it would be over quickly. Many people eagerly joined the army to gain glory for their homelands. Few imagined the true horror the following years would bring.

*Above:* Soldiers march toward the front lines. Many common people joined the armed forces, thinking it would be a short war filled with romance and adventure.
*Below:* German military leaders discuss strategy on the battlefield.

# A FAMILY AFFAIR

**ONE OF THE ODD THINGS** about World War I was that members of the same family ruled most of the countries involved. Germany's Kaiser Wilhelm II was a cousin to both Russia's Tsar Nicholas II and England's King George V. Most of the rulers of Europe were either close relatives or related to each other by marriage.

Britain's Queen Victoria was the grandmother to all the royal cousins. She arranged marriages of her children and grandchildren among the different monarchies of Europe. Queen Victoria believed that by keeping rulers within the same family, the countries of Europe would be less likely to go to war against each other. She turned out to be tragically wrong.

The royal cousins bickered and fought, as many families do. Unlike most families, however, the royal families of Europe had huge armies to command. The cousins formed alliances with and against each other. They bickered and fought over colonies in Asia and Africa.

Kaiser Wilhelm wanted his country to have as powerful a navy as his English cousin, King George V. In 1906, Great Britain produced a new kind of battleship, the first of which was called the HMS *Dreadnought*. It was a huge warship, with 10 12-inch (30-cm) guns. It was fast and powerful, and made every other battleship obsolete. Because Great Britain is an island country, it saw the development of *Dreadnought*-class battleships as necessary to its very survival. Kaiser Wilhelm saw it differently; as the ruler of an emerging superpower, he wanted Germany to be equal to the rest of

*Above:* Germany's Kaiser Wilhelm II.

Europe in every way, especially when it came to the military. Kaiser Wilhelm ordered the German navy to produce its own version of *Dreadnought*-class battleships. By 1914, Germany and Great Britain, and to a lesser extent France, were deeply involved in a naval arms race. This added to the tension and paranoia that filled the politics of the early twentieth century.

By 1914, the family rivalry of the royal cousins, together with intense feelings of national pride and jealousy, boiled over when Europe's armies mobilized and went to war.

*Left:* Russia's Tsar Nicholas II (left) and Great Britain's King George V (right)

# Sarajevo: Lighting the Fuse

**FORWARD!**

**Forward to Victory**

**ENLIST NOW**

*Above:* A poster urging men to join the armed forces
*Far right:* Austria-Hungary's Archduke Franz Ferdinand is assassinated in Sarajevo.

**AT THE TURN** of the twentieth century, the world seemed peaceful and prosperous. But the countries of Europe were ready for war. They had built huge, modern armies with advanced weapons. All the major powers had devised war plans to deal with their enemies. The planning, the men, and the equipment were all in place. All that was needed was an excuse to go to war.

The tiny nations of the Balkans, in southeastern Europe, had a history of being invaded and ruled by their neighbors. Austria-Hungary, Turkey, and Russia often fought wars over the area. The world seldom seemed to take notice because the Balkans were so out-of-the-way and seemingly unimportant.

To the people of the Balkans, however, the continual invasion by outsiders had become intolerable. Many people in the Balkan country of Serbia dreamed of ousting the invaders, getting rid of the monarchy, and forming a union of all the Balkan countries into one Slavic nation.

A secret society sprang up in Serbia called the Black Hand. The Black Hand was a small group of assassins, mostly students and former Serbian army officers. These radical terrorists were trained in firearms and bombmaking.

Bosnia-Herzegovina was a Balkan country, recently acquired as part of the Austro-Hungarian Empire. Members of the Serbian Black Hand hated this fact, and would resort to terrorism to fight for the country's freedom from imperial rule.

On June 28, 1914, Archduke Franz Ferdinand, heir apparent to the throne of Austria-Hungary, paid a visit to the capital of his country's newest province. He arrived in Sarajevo with his wife, Sophie, and began a tour of the city.

*Above:* Archduke Franz Ferdinand and his wife, Sophie, leave the residence of the governor of Bosnia-Herzegovina, in Sarajevo.

Waiting along the parade route were several Black Hand assassins. Security for the archduke was light, even though he was travelling in an open-air limousine. As the motorcade drove past, one of the assassins fumbled the controls of his bomb and failed to throw it in time. Another assassin hurled a grenade at Archduke Ferdinand's car. Instead of exploding right away, it bounced off the rear canopy and landed under the car following directly behind. The explosion injured several people, but the archduke's car sped off.

Dejected, the remaining assassins split up. One of them, Gavrilo Princip, went to an outdoor café and ordered a cup of coffee as he tried to think of what to do next.

After a reception at Sarajevo's town hall, Archduke Ferdinand made a change in his plans. He wanted to go to the military hospital to visit those who had been injured in the first assassination attempt.

As they wound through the narrow streets, the archduke's driver got lost and took a wrong turn down a side street. He stopped the car and tried to back up, but a large crowd behind the vehicle forced him to go very slowly. He eventually had to stop—right in front of the café where Gavrilo Princip, the Black Hand assassin, was drinking his coffee.

*Below:* Archduke Franz Ferdinand, and his wife Sophie, one hour before being shot and killed by Gavrilo Princip as they drove through the streets of Sarajevo.

*Above:* Gavrilo Princip is arrested moments after shooting and killing Archduke Ferdinand and his wife Sophie. Princip was too young to face the death penalty. He died four years later in prison.

Seeing his chance, Princip leapt up onto the running board of the limousine and fired three shots from his revolver at point-blank range. His first shot hit Sophie in the stomach, while his second shot hit Archduke Ferdinand in the neck. His third shot missed, but the damage was already done. Blood was everywhere, and in minutes both the archduke and his wife were dead.

Princip and his accomplices were quickly captured and later put on trial. Because he was under the legal age for execution, Princip was sentenced to 20 years in prison. He died four years later of tuberculosis. On the wall of his cell, Princip had scratched these lines:

*Our ghosts will walk through Vienna*
*And roam through the palace*
*Frightening the lords.*

Princip thought he had struck a blow for freedom for Serbia and the Balkans, but instead the Black Hand had set in motion the events that led to World War I.

Austria-Hungary, outraged at the atrocity committed by the assassins, made harsh demands of Serbia. The government of Serbia seemed eager to find a way out of the crisis, but Austria-Hungary ignored the peace offerings and declared war on July 28. The alliance agreements between the superpowers were then triggered as one country after another declared war. As the horrifying events of 1914 unfolded, Sir Edward Grey, the British Foreign Secretary, said in despair, "The lamps are going out all over Europe."

The crisis in the Balkans, the collection of tiny countries the major European powers seemed to foolishly overlook, had plunged civilization into the madness that became known as World War I.

*Below:* After months of battle, little is left at this street corner in Poelcappelle, Belgium, except the shell of a damaged tank.

# TIMELINE

1906 *February:* HMS *Dreadnought* is launched by Great Britain, beginning a worldwide naval arms race.

1914 *June 28:* Austria-Hungary's Archduke Franz Ferdinand is assassinated by a Serbian nationalist while touring Sarajevo, the capital of Bosnia-Herzegovina.

1914 *August:* World War I begins as German armed forces invade Belgium and France. Most of Europe, including Great Britain and Russia, soon enters the war.

1914 *August 26-31:* Russia suffers a major defeat at the Battle of Tannenberg.

1914 *September 9-14:* Second massive Russian defeat, this time at the Battle of the Masurian Lakes.

1915 Turkish forces slaughter ethnic Armenians living within the Ottoman Empire. The Turkish government accuses the Armenians of helping the Russians. Casualty totals vary widely, with estimates between 800,000 and 2 million Armenians killed.

1915 *Spring:* German Zeppelins launch bombing raids over English cities.

1915 *April 22:* Germans are first to use lethal poison gas on a large scale during the Battle of Ypres.

1915 *May 7:* A German U-boat sinks the unarmed British passenger liner *Lusitania*, killing 1,198 people, including 128 Americans. The American public is outraged, but President Wilson manages to keep the U.S. neutral.

1916 *February 21-December 18:* The Battle of Verdun. Nearly one million soldiers are killed or wounded.

1916 *June 24-November 13:* The Battle of the Somme costs approximately 1.25 million casualties. On the first day of the infantry attack, July 1, British forces suffered a staggering 60,000 casualties, including 20,000 dead, the largest single-day casualty total in British military history. Many troops are killed by a new battlefield weapon, the machine gun.

1917 *January 31:* Germany declares unrestricted submarine warfare, outraging the American public.

1917 *March 12:* The Russian Revolution overthrows Tsar Nicholas II.

1917 *April 6:* The United States declares war on Germany.

1917 *November:* Tanks are used for the first time on a large scale at the Battle of Cambrai. And on November 7, Russia is taken over by Lenin's communist government during the Bolshevik Revolution.

1917 *December 15:* Russia's Bolshevik government agrees to a separate peace with Germany, taking Russia out of the war.

1918 *March 21-July 19:* Germany mounts five "Ludendorff offensives" against strengthening Allied forces. The attacks are costly to both sides, but Germany fails to crush the Allied armies.

1918 *May 30-June 17:* American forces are successful against the Germans at Chateau-Thierry and Belleau Wood.

1918 *September 26-November 11:* French and American forces launch the successful Meuse-Argonne Offensive.

1918 *September 27-October 17:* British forces break through the Hindenburg Line in several places.

1918 *November 11:* Armistice Day. Fighting stops at 11:00 A.M.

1919 *May 7-June 28:* The Treaty of Versailles is written and signed.

# GLOSSARY

**ALLIES**
Great Britain, France, and Russia formed the Allies in 1914 at the outbreak of World War I. Japan also joined the Allies, but played a minor role. Russia dropped out of the war in 1917. Italy joined the Allies in 1916, followed by the United States in 1917.

**CASUALTIES**
Soldiers killed or wounded in battle.

**CENTRAL POWERS**
During World War I, the Central Powers included Germany, Austria-Hungary, and Turkey. Bulgaria also joined the Central Powers later in the war.

**COLONY**
A country or group of people controlled politically by a more powerful nation, which is often in a distant land.

**FRANCO-PRUSSIAN WAR**
The Franco-Prussian War was fought between 1870-1871. It was a huge victory for the Prussians, and eventually led to a united Germany. The war was a major defeat for the French, who lost the industry-rich provinces of Alsace-Lorraine. The war's outcome heavily influenced the bitterness and paranoia that led to the outbreak of World War I.

**MOBILIZATION**
Mobilization occurs when a country's armed forces prepare for war. Mobilization is a very complicated and expensive process. Once an army is mobilized, it is very difficult to stop a war from breaking out.

**MONARCHY**
A monarchy is a form of government in which a country is ruled by a king or queen. Unlike a democracy, monarchs are born into power. They are not voted into office by a country's citizens.

### NATIONALISM

Having a patriotic devotion to one's country. Nationalism can sometimes be taken too far, creating a blind patriotism that is excessive and narrow minded.

### NAZI

A member of the National Socialist German Workers' Party. The Nazi political party, led by Adolf Hitler, a World War I veteran, controlled Germany from 1933 until the end of World War II, in 1945.

### SEVEN WEEKS WAR

The Seven Weeks War is also known as the Austro-Prussian War. It was fought in 1866 between Prussia and Italy against Austria and its allies. The Prussians, led by Otto von Bismarck, easily defeated the Austrian forces.

### TRIPLE ALLIANCE

A military alliance between Germany, Austria-Hungary, and Italy, formed at the end of the nineteenth century. During World War I, Italy rejected the alliance, eventually siding with the Allies against Germany and Austria-Hungary.

### TRIPLE ENTENTE

A military alliance between Great Britain, Russia, and France. The Triple Entente was formed in 1904 in order to counter the Triple Alliance between Germany, Austria-Hungary, and Italy.

### WESTERN FRONT

Established by December 1914, the Western Front was a network of trenches that stretched across eastern France and a section of western Belgium. The Western Front ran approximately 400 miles (645 km), reaching from the North Sea to the border of Switzerland.

# WEB SITES

Would you like to learn more about the causes of World War I? Please visit **www.abdopub.com** to find up-to-date Web site links. These links are routinely monitored and updated to provide the most current information available.

# INDEX